TAKE THE
LIMITS
OFF

Developing Positive Attitudes
For Successful Living

SONIA WHITLOCK
Motivational Speaker & Life Coach

ISBN: 978-0-578-29963-1 (Paperback)

Front cover image by Kamaljeet Singh
Book design by Kamaljeet Singh

Printed the United States of America.

Author's Contact
Good-Wood, Tobago West Indies
Tel:1-868-380-1300
Email: soniawhitlock06@gmail.com

Disclaimer: The publisher and the authors do not make any guarantee or other promise as to any results that may be obtained from using the content of this book. This publication is meant as a source of valuable information for the reader, however it is not meant as a substitute for direct expert assistance. If such level of assistance is required, the services of a competent professional should be sought.

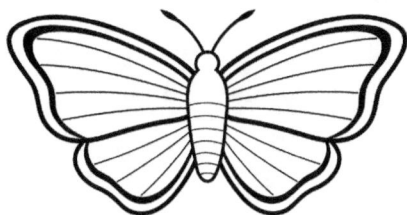

Dedication

I want to dedicate this book to the memory of my father,
the late Wilton Nancis. It is also dedicated in tribute of my mother,
Roselyn Nancis, whose love and spiritual upbringing has
defined me into becoming a God-fearing and anointed
woman of excellence and integrity.

And to all of you women whose lives I was able to touch or
in any way transformed; to women around the world who are
incarcerated by fear, rejection, abandonment, depression,
guilt, shame, anger, abuse, and oppression; those
who are broken in spirit and are at the threshold of a fresh start;
those who are ready to catapult into a season of greatness…
to all of you, may you come into awareness of all that
God has created you to be - fulfilling your
divine purpose and destiny.

Table Of Contents

What People are Saying

Sonia brings to the pages of this book, what she ministers to her congregation weekly – a message of hope, reconciliations, strength, love, forgiveness, and resilience. It is the true story of her life – examples that we can all use to help us grow and flourish. I encourage everyone reading to pay very close attention to the lessons, to reflect on what aspects are applicable to our lives, and to use them as stepping stones to ensure that you *Take the Limits Off*!

Dr. Faith B. Yisrael
Assemblyman & Secretary of Health
Wellness & Social Protection
Tobago House of Assembly

Are you familiar with the feeling of not just facing your fears but succeeding? The goosebumps you get when your imagination makes you feel invincible and your confident creative juices flow invoking a "giant inkling " where you know no limits? This is what this book gives! Not only is it utterly motivating, but it gives hope against all odds, which is incredibly comforting as it discusses human relationships in relation to biblical perspectives.

Sonia Whitlock is the personification of first-rate echelon, blended with matter-of-fact that creates the perfect recipe for the principles on which this book was written. She is riddled with real life experiences, coupled with her training in psychology and counseling, she includes interesting anecdotes from her personal life. I am guilty of fumbling through the uncertainties of life; however, I am ably assisted by the emphasis on relying on God via this Self-Help-Oriented Guide. This read is thoroughly enjoyable. Its concepts are clear and profound and is a great starting point and launch pad for transforming lives via personal introspection once the precepts are digested and internalized.

Keyler Whitlock-St. Hillaire B.S (Behavioral Sciences)
Counselor & Business Entrepreneur

Rev. Sonia Whitlock is both graceful and profound in her writing. She reminds us provocatively that we are not to allow people and circumstances to confine or limit us in any such way that it diminishes our purpose. She compels us to question ourselves actively about who we are at every step of our journey. Just like the caterpillar metamorphoses into a butterfly, so too are we required to transmogrify and transmute from our fallen nature into who God has called and purposed us to be. She reminds us that it is God's approval that is sovereign not man's so we can fearlessly look at our past blunders and declare "So what!"

This book is the real deal. If you are searching for a timely affirmation on how you can overthrow your Philistine and take a stand for yourself, then look no further. Get ready to weather your storms and embrace your wilderness experiences because God will only move when you are ready to be moved.

WARNING: You are about to be blessed!

Josanne Rojas
Author and Kingdom Comrade

Foreword

My mind reflects on my personal, professional, and spiritual development as a young woman through the years. I always enjoyed observing and learning from influential women in my Tobago community. Pastor Sonia Whitlock always stood out. I was first mesmerized by her captivating vocals and the way in which she managed her magical voice. She commanded the room, she was powerful – yet graceful, strong – but sweet. She was a rare diamond, one of a kind and she carried herself like she knew it. I loved to see her, loved to hear her speak, and most of all, I looked forward to our little talks as she always showered me with pearls of wisdom. She often encouraged me to stand in my truth, walk in my purpose, and claim my peace through Jesus.

Interestingly we share the same mantra. I often say, "What people say about me is none of my business, I know who I am and who God has created me to be, so all the nasty criticisms and baseless chatter amounts to nothing, precious nothings." Pastor Whitlock has a more eloquent and sophisticated way of expressing the same sentiment. She likes to say, "What matters is not what others say or think about you – it is what God says about you that matters; and it is only the plans and purpose of God for your life that will prevail." She is a lady after my own heart. She is real. She is honest. She is fearless and she is frank. This was a woman to watch, a lady to emulate, and a Kingdom ambassador worthy of recognition, reverence, and respect.

Pastor Whitlock's work really took flight as she began ministering to the people of Tobago through the Sanctuary of Praise Worship Tabernacle. She takes keen interest in coaching and mentoring women and girls, and she takes her precious time to make sure that others feel valued by her and loved by God. She is compassionate and caring to any and everyone. Sounds cliché, but this is genuinely who she is. She was created with a beautiful gift to empower and she remains committed to her duty to inspire and lift as she climbs.

Take the Limits Off provides a riveting account of Pastor Whitlock's life, baring it all, pointedly, passionately, and purposefully as she was ordained to be. She has had her fair share of ups and downs, failures and triumphs, mortification and jubilation, but God has kept her through it all. She is not ashamed of her past, and she is certainly not afraid to share the details, dish out the dirt, and tell you as it is. The turbulence in her life's journey has helped mold her into the divine diva she is today. *Take the Limits Off* teaches us to embrace every step of our voyage to victory, wearing our scars as badges of honour, and sharing our testimonies of God's promises to give us beauty for ashes and strength for tears.

This is her story, this is your story, this is our story. Each chapter reminds us of God's promise to save, to keep, and to satisfy. Each account shared enlightens us as womenfolk, that we all go through similar trials; and as much as we may feel alone in the valley of dry bones, there's always someone like Pastor Whitlock who is ready to step in and be a rock, a shoulder to lean on, a guiding light, and a good shepherd. There will always be a warrior like her to lead us out of our many dungeons of deceit, deception, humiliation, depression, darkness, and distress. This book is a bare witness of God's promise to heal the sick, comfort the broken-hearted, be a tower of strength for the weak, and most importantly to pick us up, turn us around, and place our feet on higher ground. This is Kingdom business, and thanks to Pastor Sonia Whitlock, I'm here for all of it.

She takes us into her family, her marriage, her childhood, and her ministry, carefully dissecting the many facets of her role as a lady in leadership, who took no short-cuts and who had to labour and learn to attain unimaginable levels of success in her personal and professional life; most uniquely in her personal walk with Christ.

Take the Limits Off encourages us to hand all our troubles over to God, to pray ceaselessly, and to watch and pray in the process. This profoundly, genuine, and beautiful rendition calls on us to lay down our pride, worries, fears and shame, allowing us to make room for God to enter and be all that He is.

This is not just a book, this is an experience. *Take the Limits Off* will change your life, and open new doors toward healing, spiritual growth, and prosperity in Christ. This book is for the lady who is ready to walk in her true purpose and bask in the glory of God; lovingly, limitlessly, confidently, and courageously. This book is dedicated to the ladies who are ready to soar.

What an honour and privilege it is to be guided by Pastor Sonia, as we stand in the promise and majesty of our Creator and finally *Take the Limits Off*!

Shamfa Ashaki Cudjoe
Minister of Sport and Community Development
Member of Parliament for Tobago West

Preface

My inspiration, to write this book, came from my spiritual and personal experiences. The storms of my life have inspired and taught me how to use every negative escapade as stepping stones to launch me into greater. The devastating events of my past have stimulated me to break through the external and internal pressures of life. It was during these times of adversity I found my true identity in Christ.

If you are reading the words on this page may I say to you – This is your season to arise and shine. It's time to smile again. It's time to get your groove back! If you stay stuck in the past, you will miss what's ahead of you. Allow me to say to you that I will be the first to admit that the lessons I have learned in life will last throughout my lifetime. It was during these difficult times I realized that my pit experiences eventually helped me to embrace the qualities and attributes I possessed. However, initially because of my loss of self, I was opposed to change. Thankfully, I had an epiphany that nothing changes if nothing changes; and I want to implore you - starting today, why not be the change you want to see.

Throughout my sojourn, I've had an overwhelming passion for ministering and touching the lives of hurting women and adolescent girls. As I reflect over my life working as a Motivational Speaker, Life Coach, Counsellor, and Pastor, I have been afforded countless opportunities to support and mentor women from all ethnic backgrounds to navigate their way through their issues, challenges, and painful experiences.

This book is a must read. The stories I have shared are testimonies drawn from my encounters in life. I would like to challenge you to read every chapter. Make it a daily appointment on your schedule. My prayer for you is that as you read this book, you are able to face and conquer whatever painful obstacles and roadblocks you have encountered in the past. My desire for you is that you break free from your victim mentality and release yourself from the guilt, shame, and past regrets. May God give you the grace of releasing where you have been so you can embrace what God has in store for you.

Ladies, it's time to release the emotional scars of fear, anxiety, abuse, rejection, and loneliness that you have carried for so long. And never relinquish who God created you to be by chasing a personality that was not orchestrated by God for your life. You are fearfully and wonderfully made by God. You've got what it takes! You've got class! You are witty and smart! It's time to get your groove back!

I was compelled to write this book, *Take the Limits Off*, as I reflected over my life and the series of hurt, pain, abuse, betrayal, rejection, deception, disappointments, and regrets I endured in my quest to fulfill my destiny. There was a strong conviction by the Holy Spirit compelling me to share my testimony with women; encouraging them to push past their hurt and the pain.

As I wrote with you in mind, I often prayed that you would experience the healing, restoration, hope, and peace that comes from unveiling God's plan for your life. The themes of this book are blended with my personal life experiences intertwined with biblical scriptures, positive affirmations, and personal reflections which will transform your life. I am confident that your life will be remodeled just as my life has found new meaning.

In *Take the Limits Off*, each chapter focuses on life experiences and spiritual principles that will support you in examining, exploring, and healing your broken emotions. The emphasis of this book is about learning to forgive yourself from the mistakes of the past. It empowers you to create atmospheres that are conducive to the realization of fulfilling your purpose and developing a relationship with Jesus Christ. The chapters are presented in an order that will inspire and motivate you to discover the treasured seeds of greatness that God has placed within you.

At the end of each chapter, I have included positive declarations, prayers, and personal reflections designed to liberate and give you spiritual motivation. There are times you will be asked to write about valuable insights, spiritual convictions, and lessons you have learned. I would also recommend that you keep a journal to make entries that will enhance your personal and spiritual self-improvement as you embark on this healing process.

My desire is for you to follow God's divine destiny for your life and stay in your purpose. Take the limits off God! Remove the hindrances and run the course. Whatever you do, keep pressing. Keep believing. Shake off your past. It's not how you start that counts it's how you finish. Dare to finish strong. No matter how good, or bad, your life is, every circumstance can change for the best if you learn how to *Take the Limits Off!*

Introduction

Have you ever struggled finding your identity? You're doing everything in your power to discover who you are and remove the limitations of your thoughts, words, and actions; but due to the heaviness of your past lurking as shadows of your present, you're at a loss of where to even begin. Then, this book is for you, and it's designed to propel, empower, motivate, and encourage you to take the action needed to turn your possibilities into realities. In essence, you will be able to develop an unquenchable passion to catapult into your destiny.

Take the Limits Off, was first penned approximately eight years ago, and it contains the most important lessons about life that I have learned during my own transformative, emotional, and spiritual journey over the last thirty-six years. As we enter this new millennium, we are living during a very potent time… ripened with opportunities for tremendous growth and awakening. May I invite you to walk with me and take the most rewarding adventure of your life, a journey that will lead you back to the core of your sense of self.

There came a time when I had to face the truth about myself. And it was during these times, I made a conscious decision that it was time to step up and step out of my comfort zone – step out of the mire of sin and pursue my God-given purpose. In your voyage of life, there are times you may have strayed from the Call of God upon your life. In spite of your flaws and imperfections, God will channel your life in the right direction. God saw the best in you when everyone around could only see the worst in you. He considered the times you became frustrated, rebellious, and disobedient. He imputed your victories and failures. Yes! He intentionally symphonizes your life so that His purpose for your life will be accomplished.

There are so many individuals who choose to stay where they are; physically, mentally and emotionally suffering in silence because they dare not break free from their past. As human beings, we are trained to resist that which is difficult and ignore that which is spiritual. We go through wilderness experiences that help bring true purpose and meaning of life. I hear you asking, "Sonia, wilderness experiences?" Yes, wilderness experiences are those experiences that compels you to question who you are, recognize what you want, and determine what you are willing to do regarding your achievements in life.

May I say to you, you must find the strength within to allow your desert experiences to thrust you into your purpose?

What are the demands on your life in which you have allowed that God has never planned for your life?

What past failures have you allowed to obscure your vision of your God-ordained future?

What condemnations have you let plague and influence you to the point that it diminished your self-value and self-worth?

I am of the firm belief that it is the will and desire of God that every human being commit and dedicate ourselves to maximizing our potential in the midst of life's challenges. It is of uttermost importance that you come to terms with these questions because they are related to your destiny. You were created by God to be peculiar, special, priceless, irreplaceable, and unique. You are fearfully and wonderfully made by God.

We all have a picture of how we thought our lives should be, but if we are honest with ourselves, we have to admit that our lives look very different from that picture. It doesn't matter where you are in life. Whether you, or someone you know, has been incapacitated by childhood adversity, an unsavory memory of the past, a failed relationship, or even bad choices that are now causing a wellspring of anguish and bitterness... God wants to bring you to a place of rest; where there are no hurts or hang-ups. God wants to bring you to a place of being totally surrendered to Him. Many women become caught up in who they think they should be, not who they were created to be. May I say to you ladies that you are sabotaging yourself from all God has in store for you.

Throughout my journey, I have had an overwhelming passion for ministering and touching the lives of hurting, and abused, adolescent girls and women. When other people would have treated them as an outcast, I always extended a hand of love and mercy. Perhaps it is because I've had my share of life's ups and downs. Understand this, when you have endured suffering as a good soldier, it cushions you to be equipped to relate to other people's pain. God positioned me in a ministry that cares for hurting and unchurched people to the extent that when I minister, I am brought to tears. I can relate to (and feel) my audience's brokenness because it reminds me of my past.

To those of you who are struggling with the mistakes of your past, know this, if you have been resilient enough to weather the hurts in your life, rest assured that this too shall pass. For some of you, you may have experienced turbulences of internal pressures that have overwhelmed you, but you have learned along the journey to take refuge in the Lord. I salute you. And yes – you are in it to win it!

As women, we must become intentional and maximize our potential, from within, while on our quest to fulfil our destiny. Whether you are a single mother, an astute businesswoman, or at your wits end to keep your marriage together; the time has come for you to release your past, forgive yourself, relinquish everything that's been holding you back, and step into the woman God has called you to be. Your designated moment has come, and it's time for you to get ready to step into your new level of destiny.

Note from the Author

Ladies, as women we are susceptible to make mistakes. We are forced to improvise whether we like it or not. *Take the Limits Off* is a life transforming journey to equip women to reclaim the pieces of self that have been lost in the wrestle to validate their own sense of worth. You are holding this book in your hands, and reading these words, because you are scheduled for a profound shift. Something good is about to happen to you. Can't you feel it? A metamorphosis is about to take place!

Have you ever experienced a sudden change in your life that leaves the plans for your life in a messed-up state? Have you ever experienced your integrity and reputation being questioned? Have you ever made a decision that seemed correct at the time, but now you deeply regret? Have you ever felt embittered to the very depths of your soul (to the extent that your spirit was broken)? Have you ever had to tango with God when every avenue you turned to for help was only closed doors? Have you ever felt the need to change your name due to the drama surrounding you and your family?

If you answered yes to any of those questions, trust me, I understand. I've been around long enough and have lost enough to know that we all experience losses in our lives at one point of time or the other. Maybe your husband walked out on you. Or maybe you are experiencing relational issues. Maybe you've even been disappointed by a friend? Whether you weren't raised by your parents who should have deposited positive values in your life, or you've inherited attitudes of defeat, mediocrity, addictions, and negativity – I've been there.

I am aware that you have experienced some unfair things in the past that have made your life difficult, but you do not have to stay the way you are. The time has come for you to break free from things that has held you back in the past. If you feel uncomfortable with where you are in life, the wind of change is blowing. "It's time for joy, not sorrow; it's time for beauty, not ashes; it's time for you to be all that God created you to be".

I invite you to read with an open mind and an open heart, and with the intension of receiving the messages that are meant just for you. Let the words penetrate deep into your spirit. I guarantee you that the life changing revelation of *Take the Limits Off* will make you smile, cry, think, forgive, and transform your life. It is my prayer that this book will liberate, heal, transform, and empower women to break free from their past; and to discover the true essence of their value, worth, and power.

Dearly beloved, are you ready to join me on this journey to becoming a better you?

Penned with Love and Affection,
Sonia Whitlock

1 Chapter

Pick Yourself Up and Go Again

"Remember not the former things, nor consider the things of old.
Behold, I am doing a new thing; now it springs forth,
do you not perceive it? I will make a way in the wilderness
and rivers in the desert".
Isaiah 43:18-19

I say to you today, it does not matter what you have been through, or what has happened to you – it does not even matter what other people have done or have said about you. Maybe you have been ostracized, criticized, abused, misused, and ridiculed. You are a brand of what is inside of you, and who is in you. You have the capability to be all that you are conceived to be. I dare you to never give up on accomplishing your dreams. Dream until your dreams come true. No matter what you face in life, pick yourself up and go again. I grew up in a home where my parents instilled godly principles in me. I was taught that the secret to success is that you never give up no matter how hard the challenges are.

At a very young age, I encountered relationships that introduced me to criticism and judgment. I did not know how to process the negative accusations hurled at me, as such, I became withdrawn and often wished

I could become invisible to avoid being hurt. What I quickly learned is that in our journey through life, we all will encounter many people who will attempt to tear us down or break our spirit. Beloved, don't allow anyone's criticism and judgment to define who you are. If people refuse to look at you in a new light, if all they can see are your failures and the mistakes you have made, it's time to let them go! When life seems to beat you down, I dare you to PICK YOURSELF UP AND GO AGAIN!

A woman does not just wake up one day with the belief that she cannot stand the way she looks or the life she has lived. There was a time in my life when I had messed up drastically. During this time of experimentation, labels and lies were placed on me by people. Actually, on numerous occasions I felt that I did not have the strength and power to overcome the temptations which life presented to me. I grew up strongly convinced that I was inferior, and therefore, I tried to win the approval of others. Not anymore! Gone are those days. I have come to realize that mistakes are stepping stones to launch you into your greatness. There will be occasions when trouble enters our lives, and we cannot do anything to avoid them. I need for you to understand that they are there for a reason. To build character, to humble you, and to strengthen your faith and trust in God. I deem these times as "wilderness" periods.

May I ask you this pertinent question, "What is your wilderness?" Is it your marriage? Your career? Your ministry? Your family? Is it your health?

The children of Israel's assignment were to walk through the wilderness into the promised land which was a place of victory and abundance. God never intended for them to remain in the wilderness; His plan was for them to pass through it unharmed. Likewise, He has a plan for you in your wilderness. No matter what pain you experience in life, see it as a shift toward something better. Remember you are equipped to handle it!

If you believe the labels and lies that are put on you by people, you will not have the power necessary to live a successful life. People will always try to define "who" you are by what you do; including how you dress, how you speak, how you act, and by your past. It is time for us to stop living up to other people's expectations. If I had permitted my failures (or what seemed to me at the time to be a lack of success) to discourage me, I cannot see any way in which I would ever have made progress. There comes a time when you need to say, "Enough is enough!" and respect yourself enough to walk away from anything or anyone that's detrimental to your physical and spiritual progress. Life is too short to maintain toxic relationships!

Perhaps some of you are thinking of giving up. Some of you feel like quitting. Some of you might be asking, "Why me?" You may be at the verge of a break down. I hear you saying, "I am fed-up of life and living. I am tired mentally and physically. What's the use!" Well I have come by to encourage you to keep running the race. There is no need for you to drop the baton. *Do not get weary in well doing, for God gives power to the faint, and to him who has no might he increases strength, but they who wait for the LORD shall renew their strength; they shall mount up with wings like eagles; they shall run and not be weary; they shall walk and not faint. (Isaiah 40:30-31)*

The time has come for you to dust yourself off and embrace your diverseness. That is where you will find your value. There were times in my life when I was deeply hurt. As a woman I felt disparage and undermined. I felt like I had lost my identity and self-worth. I have two words for you to use when people bring your past to remembrance. "SO, WHAT!" The next time someone says, "You are a loser, you will never amount to anything" and others accuse you by saying, "Look at the life you led," respond "SO, WHAT!" In God's eyes your past has nothing to do with your future!

Each time you allow the enemy to frustrate you with your past failures, you are telling him that you miss what you had. So, what if I messed up! So, what if he left me! So what if I lost the car! So, what? Allow me to say to you, "God will vindicate your cause." He promised never to leave you nor forsake you, but to be with you even until the end. However, for your total healing and restoration, an act of purification must take place. You must be able to forgive and love again!

Whilst we are on the topic of love. Permit me to ask, what are the things that have taken you away from your first love for God?

After David's shameful sin with Bathsheba, he went to God and cried out in desperation for God's help. *Create in me a clean heart O God, and renew a right spirit within me. Cast me not away from your presence and take not your Holy Spirit from me. (Psalms 51:10-11.)*

What you need to understand is for you to be totally free from the bondage of sin, you must first admit that you have sinned and come short of God's glory. Living in denial will not solve the problem; it only makes matters worst. David openly acknowledged his sin, picked up the pieces of his life, and came out with a resounding victory.

Let me tell you the secret that has led me to being successful. My strength lied solely in God and in my tenacity. The next time you feel as though you want to give up, speak to yourself. Ask yourself, "Will this matter a year from now?" Quit sweating over petty stuff! As I look back on my life, I realize that every time I thought I was being rejected from something good, I was actually being redirected to something better. Now, I hope that you are on your way to change. Do not allow your dreams to die because you refuse to release yourself from your past. You need to push your way through and focus on the dreams and goals you've set for yourself in the natural and especially the spiritual. God is ready to use you mightily to bring Glory to His name, but He can't do it if you are unwilling to relinquish that which tried to take you out.

How senseless it would be for you to go through nine months of pregnancy, and when it is time to give birth, you refuse to push. Listen, it would make absolutely no sense to go through all those sleepless nights, the waiting, the pain, the stirring of life inside your womb, only to think you don't have the power within you to finish the job when the time finally comes. Snap out of that negative mindset, Sis! You have everything you need inside of you to give birth to your destiny! It is time to push with everything you've got. Without fail, you must continuously speak life to yourself. You must constantly remind yourself of who you are. Yes! *Death and life lie in the power of your and it is only those who love it will eat its fruits. (Proverbs 18:21)*

When your dreams are shattered, do not quit. What many people don't understand as well, is that failure is not the opposite of success. Contrary to popular belief, failure is in fact something that must take place on the road to success. It is what stretches us and helps us grow. It's what reminds us that we need Jesus to see us through, that we can't do anything without His mighty hand being in it. Quitting is the opposite of success. Therefore, when things get tough, do not throw in the towel. That is the time you need to persevere. That is the time you need to persist. The time you need to show determination and stand your ground! When your business is failing, that is not the end of the road! In fact, there is a lesson you will need to learn during that test. When your marriage or health begins to deteriorate, that is not your destiny. Your destiny is in Christ!

Now are you ready to push toward your future? There is no stopping you now! Do not let the past obscure your vision. Focus! You are about to give birth. Push! But be careful, – you do not want any complications! Inhale; exhale! Push! Now here it comes. Wow! You have just given birth to a new life in Christ Jesus… a new you! *Any man in Christ is a new creature, old things are passed away, behold all things have become new. (2 Corinthians 5:17)*.

Doesn't it feel good to let go of the past? Can you feel the release of your pain? Cry if you may – that's fine – tears are a language God understands. Yes! You can smile again. The storm is over! Here comes new life. You are on your way to fulfilling destiny!

Walk Into Your Season!

This song *"No More"* was written by my son Keylon Whitlock, it summarizes in essence what was highlighted in the chapter.

NO MORE
By Keylon Whitlock

No more lies, no more pain, no more dwelling on my past.
Now I'm wise, now I'm strong and with you Lord I can go on.
For with you I have security, and you said with me you'll stay.
I'm promised a life of prosperity and it's starting from today.

CHORUS

No more, no more running, no more hiding - No
No more, no more believing I'm not worth it - No
I finally found the strength I need to go on and I found it in the Lord.

No more conflict, no more stress, now I'm holding on to Jesus.
Cause He is life and He's love, and it's He who is my focus
For with you I have security, and you said with me you'll stay.
I'm promised a life of prosperity and it's starting from today.

BRIDGE

Now I'm changed, now I'm new, I'm not going back no-way.
I will win and not lose, for his Word is life.
For with you I have security, and you said with me you'll stay.
I'm promised a life of prosperity and it's starting from today.

CHORUS

No more, no more running, no more hiding - No
No more, no more believing I'm not worth it - No
I finally found the strength I need to go on and I found it in the Lord.

Soul Searching & Inventory Exercise

Pick Yourself Up and Go Again

There is a myriad of benefits to journaling. Some benefits include achieving your goals, identifying areas for improvement, and tracking your personal progress or growth. Below are questions that will help you search your soul and take a personal inventory of yourself.

Part One

What is your current wilderness?

_____

_____

_____

_____

_____

How did this become your wilderness?

_____

_____

_____

_____

_____

What part do you play in this wilderness?

_____

_____

_____

_____

What actions can you take to press through your wilderness?

_____

_____

_____

_____

How committed are you to overcome your wilderness?

_____

_____

_____

_____

Part Two

Your feelings are the keys you need to tap into your experience. You can use your Journal to release, your emotions. Write your thoughts and healing experience.

What are you willing to release (i.e. thoughts, feelings, fears, and/or behaviors that relates to your past)?

What life lessons did you learn the hard way?

_____

_____

_____

_____

_____

What experience in your past you feel most angry about?

_____

_____

_____

_____

_____

_____

What aspect of your life would you like to change?

_____

_____

_____

_____

_____

How did this particular experience make you feel?

_____

_____

_____

_____

What would you do differently if you had to do it all over again?

_____

_____

_____

_____

_____

Dear God,

*I recognize that I cannot make it without you. I acknowledge that
I am a sinner.*

*Please forgive me. Heal my messed up life. Restore unto me the joy
of my Salvation, and renew a right spirit within me.
You are my life and my strength.*

*Eliminate the hurt, pain, and shame I carried around for so long.
Thank you for giving me a second chance.*

*Thank you for loving me, for saving me, and for redeeming
my life from destruction. Take control of my life in
Jesus' Name. Amen*

Chapter 2

I am an Overcomer!

God hath not given us the spirit of fear, but of power,
love, and a sound mind.
2 Timothy 1:7

Many of us live from day to day without a real sense of purpose. We know we want more out of life, but we are bombarded by rejection and fear of the unknown. Somebody pulled a fast one on you and tricked you into believing that you were not good enough; and it's unfortunate, but you believed that. The truth is they blatantly told you a lie! Now what are you going to do about it? Accept, or reject it? Think about some of the things that you've been allowing to restrict you from letting your light shine? Could it possibly be that you feel because of your past experiences you would not be respected, appreciated, or not noticed? On many occasions, we allow negative circumstances that surround us to intimidate us – causing us to quench the fire within.

During this time, we become afraid of launching out; we become boxed in by the attacks of condemnation, shame, and fear of failure. The Word of God teaches: *Perfect love will expel all fear.* (1 John 4:18)

Child of God, I need for you to understand that fear stifles your progress. It causes you to remain silent. It muffles you and can even debilitate you. Because of fear, you refuse to say what is on your mind. Don't you know by remaining silent, you quietly give people the right to do whatever they please with you? If you allow this to happen, it places you in a state of dormancy and ultimately stunts your growth.

Vividly, I remember a time in my life when I allowed fear to control me. Understand this, living in fear is a dangerous thing. You basically give control to the very people you allow to place fear in you.

In my younger days, I was often criticized for doing the right thing, and for being popular. In fear, I told myself, "The best thing for me to do is remain silent." I withdrew from everything I liked doing. It never occurred to me that I was allowing people to control every aspect of my life. I allowed their criticism to force me into a place where I felt very uncomfortable with myself and my abilities.

In my state of dormancy, I trusted the judgment of others around me, simply because I wanted to win their approval. I also started becoming an avid listener to gossip, which contaminated my thoughts and my spirit. No longer was I able to interpret things for myself. My joy, peace of mind, and hope for brighter days were all lost because I found myself placing my trust in man, as opposed to relying heavily on God.

Those who thought they knew me, would have viewed my transition from adolescent to adulthood as one of great achievement. However, I often wondered how I made it through and even asked myself that question on several occasions. At this juncture, I became very afraid at the thought of what my life had become and would become.

Let's be clear, at some point in time in life, you will experience fear. Fear is a very natural and normal response to the challenges we face in life. It is an indicator that warns us that there is something we must be cautious about. What are your deepest fears? Fear of death, losing your job, your family, a relationship, fear of taking a stand for what is right? Understand that fear of the unknown is normal, however, you must trust God during those times to ensure that the fear does not begin to control you.

The time has come for you to step up and stand out. The time has come for you to confront whatever it is that has paralyzed your progress and made you stagnant. I dare you to take courage and confront your fears. With man it is impossible, but with God, all things are possible. It is time to say good-bye to fear, intimidation, procrastination, low-self-esteem, and other complications that have caused you to be at a setback. This is your day, this is your hour, and it's time to shine again!

Why not look at yourself in the mirror and affirm, "I am fearfully and wonderfully made by God. I can do anything that I set out to do." To be an overcomer, you must learn to live fearlessly. This is the only way to truly find yourself in God. He is the way, the truth, and the life.

As I reflect over my life, it was the Word of God which guided me in my everyday actions and decision-making. I learned when faced with a dilemma, that I should not *lean on my own understanding, but in all my ways I must acknowledge God and He will direct my path.* (Proverbs 3:6)

Today, I write to a hurting mother, a lonely wife, a battered woman, and an insecure sister. I speak to a man who is at his wits end. Even though you are trained, educated, qualified, and gifted in so many ways, you have allowed what was said about you to cause you to abort your purpose.

The circumstances that have surrounded your life, and the series of hurt that you have endured over the years, have made you to feel like a nobody. Some of you are between a rock and a hard place. Your light has been blown out by the issues of life:

- ✔ Relational Issues
- ✔ Ministry Issues
- ✔ Marital Issues
- ✔ Financial Issues
- ✔ Mid-Life Crisis Issues
- ✔ Health Issues

Be thou encouraged. *The joy of the Lord is your strength.* David said, *"I will lift up mine eyes unto the hills from whence cometh my help."* (Psalm 121) Step out in faith and believe God is working things out for your good! Step into the calling you were born to live in. The sky is the limit!

I have learned that a mind focused on doubts and fears restrict you from reaching your goals. It was only when I let go and submitted so that God could take full control of my life that He led me to a life of fulfillment, joy, and peace. I dare you to take up the challenge. Whatever your fears may be; fear of failure, fear of criticism, fear of being imperfect, no matter what it is, ask the Lord to give you strength and help you deal with it!

As a matter of fact, even better, relinquish it to Jesus; all your fears, your shattered dreams, wounded heart, and your broken thoughts... all of it. By doing this, you release yourself from past hurts, criticism, failures, anger, bitterness, shame, blame, resentment and guilt.

Study these lines of scripture, carefully, as you embark on this new journey of living a surrendered life to God.

- ✔ *For I know the thoughts that I think toward you, says the Lord, thoughts of peace and not of evil, to give you a future and a hope.* (Jeremiah 29:11)

- ✔ *The steps of a good man are ordered by the Lord.*
(Psalm 37:23)

- ✔ *A man's heart plans his way, but the Lord directs his steps.*
(Proverbs 16:9)

- ✔ *Delight yourself also in the Lord, and He shall give you the desires of your heart. Commit your way to the Lord, trust also in Him, and He shall bring it to pass ... Rest in the Lord, and wait patiently for Him.* (Psalm 37:4,7)

It does not matter where you have been or what you have done, know this, Jesus loves you. He is concerned about you, and He has great plans for your life!

As you go forth I dare you to:

- Stand firm in the midst of obstacles.

- Stand firm in the midst of criticism.

- Stand firm in the midst of persecution

- Stand firm in the midst of doubt

- Stand firm in the midst of opposition

- Stand firm in the midst of difficulties

With God on your side, you will never be defeated. "Be bold and be strong for the Lord thy God is with you".

Soul Searching & Inventory Exercise

I am all that Life is!

You can choose how you will respond to all experiences; however, the goal of this exercise is to help you overcome adversity which leads to freedom, better choices, and enhances your well-being. Consider the following questions:

What challenges have you overcome?

_____

_____

_____

_____

_____

What lessons have these challenges taught you (be specific)?

_____

_____

_____

_____

_____

When have you failed?

_____

_____

_____

_____

_____

Why do you consider the(se) experience(s) to be failures?

_____

_____

_____

_____

_____

What did you learn from your failures?

_____

_____

_____

_____

_____

What actions did you take to overcome these failures?

_____

_____

_____

_____

_____

If you could change one thing about yourself, what would it be and why?

_____

_____

_____

_____

_____

Based on your past experiences, write a personal word of affirmation that will serve as a reminder that you are indeed an overcomer.

_____

_____

_____

_____

_____

Dear God,

I recognize that I cannot make it without you. I acknowledge that I am a sinner.

I come to you in the name of Jesus. You know the difficult situations I am faced with.

Your Word declares in the book of Romans 8:37 "In all these things we are more than conquerors through him that loved us".

Almighty God – Your thoughts are not my thoughts, neither your ways my ways.

Give me the strength and the courage to overcome every negative obstacle.

I feel stressed, I am worried, and unsettled. Lead me and guide me.

Fill me with love, peace, joy, kindness, goodness, gentleness and self-control. In the name of Jesus Amen.

Chapter

Speak Life - Embrace Change!

Death and life are in the power of the tongue, and those
who love it will eat its fruit."
Proverbs 18:21

Many people are driven by the need for approval. They allow the prediction of others to manipulate their lives, causing them to spend their entire lives running from regrets and hiding in their shame. If you were to describe yourself, what would you say? Don't you know that the way you feel about yourself influences what you do, and why you do everything in life? Have you ever stopped to look at the memories of when you felt great, or on top of the world? Those are the moments that prove what a wonderful and amazing human being you are? I do not know all the keys to success, but this I know, one critical key to failure is trying to please everyone.

Allow me to ask you a few thought provoking questions. What do you meditate on? Positive or empowering thoughts, affirming thoughts, or are you driven by forgiveness? What about bitterness, negativity, or unforgiveness? I have learned from experience that resentment always hurts you more than it does the person you resent. While your Goliath has moved on with life, you continue to hoard the offense in pain. Like me, you may have tried on numerous occasions to take matters into your own hands, only to mess things up even worse.

This experience drew me back to the Apostle Paul, and his life experiences which were likened "as a thorn in his flesh". During this time, I grew angry, bitter, and hostile. Most of my days were manipulated by memories of hurt and pain which sabotaged my own success. Physically, I was tired; mentally, I was drained; and spiritually, I was weak. All because I retaliated in my own strength. However, according to 2 Corinthians 12:10 "We are only strong when we are weak." It is during these times of uncertainty you need to know that amidst what you are faced with in this life, God's grace is sufficient for you. It was only when I came to the realization that the battle does not belong to me, there came a seismic shifting in the atmosphere. It was only when I truly surrendered myself completely to God, that I won the victory over my enemies.

The time has come for you to release yourself from the negative words that were spoken over your life. Even if you find yourself surrounded by what seems catastrophic, continue to speak positive declarations over your life. Know this... words carry great power. You may ask, "How can our tongue be powerful enough to produce life and death?" In the Book of Genesis, we see that in the creation story, God created everything by His spoken word. *In the beginning was the Word, and the Word was with God, and the Word was God.* (John 1:1) Further, the book of Isaiah alludes to saying, *My word that goes out from my mouth, it will not return to me empty, but will accomplish what I desire and achieve the purpose for which I sent it.* (Isaiah 55:11)

It has been my experience as a pastor, who does extensive counselling, often wrong-thinking patterns stem from childhood. On many occasions, the people who should have been nurturing us and telling us what we could become, did just the opposite. For some of us we have suffered the mental damage of evil words spoken over our lives, somebody mistreated you, somebody rejected you, somebody abused you; a parent, family member, or even your best friend, and as a result, (because you did not know better) you just let this take root.

This thought rooted itself deep into your mind and caused negative thinking to limit you from becoming all you were created to be.

Jantz, in his book, *Healing the Scars of Emotional Abuse*, stated, "Emotional abuse is so damaging because it outlives its own life span. Not only does it damage a person's self-esteem, but it also sets up a life-pattern that daily assaults the inner being." (31) In light of this, you need to re-program your mind. You need to shake off those negative messages and experiences. Our dialogue should always be positive and hopeful. I guarantee you, if you will talk to yourself in the right way, you will not only enjoy your life more, but you will rise higher to a new level of confidence, a new level of boldness. For some of us, I know it is not easy.

Maybe you are living far below your potential; feeling bad about yourself, lacking confidence, and wallowing in low self-esteem. Have you considered that it could be a result of what you are constantly speaking to yourself, or have heard from someone? Some of you may have gone through some major setbacks in life, having numerous disappointments, failures, bankruptcy, or even divorce. I say to you today, "Learn to speak life into your situation." Don't get me wrong, I am not saying to take the easy way out. I am saying that it does you no good to go around feeling condemned, disgraced, or disqualified over something that is in the past.

I know what it feels like to be opposed. When opposition comes our way, we get confused and, in most cases, we feel like quitting. I need for you to know that God is on your side; and if God be for you, no man can be against you. Having an understanding of the Word of God is the key to your survival. The Word of God declares, *Put on the whole armour of God that ye may be able to stand in stand against the wiles of the enemy. That we put on the helmet of salvation and the sword of the spirit – which is the Word of God. For when the enemy shall come in like a flood the Lord your God will lift up a standard against them.* (Ephesians 6:11 -18)

It makes no sense sitting in a corner, playing pity party with yourself. It makes no sense lying in bed hoping that you will get up and the problem will go away. You've got to GET UP! Get up from under that juniper tree, dust yourself off, and keep on moving. Yes, your friends may have forsaken you. Yes, your husband may have walked out on you. Yes, your parents may have given up on you. This is the time when you have to get your praise on! This is the time you have to open your mouth and tell the devil where to get off! This is the time when you have a take a stand and fight back with the Word of God! Jehoshaphat was told to "Stand Still" and so I say to you today, "Don't worry yourself with the enemy, don't worry with the outcome, God has it all under control! Position yourself in prayer and praise and when you have done all you can – STAND!

Whatever you are faced with today may be frightening. Know this it was not meant for your destruction, but for your Christian growth and development. Jeremiah 29:11 states, *For I know the thoughts I think towards you saith the Lord are thoughts of peace and not evil, to give you an expected end.* Who could better comfort a wife who has been through the fire, and the storm, than a woman who has been through that agony herself? Who could minister to an adolescent mother more than a woman who has walked that path? Who can best administer healing and restoration to an addict than one who battled with these same issues? The Bible says, *He comforts us in all our troubles so that we can comfort others.* (2 Corinthians 1:4)

If your desire is to be used by God, you must understand a powerful truth; the very experiences that we have resented or regretted most in our lives, or the ones we have wanted to hide and forget, are the exact experiences God wants to use to help others. They are your ministry! Remember, what we endure is unto the glory of God, our father. What you have had to endure was for all the people you were meant to bring to Christ. This is for HIS glory and non-else!

Maybe, you have been placed in a position where it seems difficult for you to get rid of the negative voices in your head. Or maybe you have entertained and digested the words of your critics and you have arrived at the conclusion that it is normal to go around feeling bad

TAKE THE LIMITS OFF

about yourself. Understand, the negative voices always seem to cry out the loudest, and if not released, they create a war on the inside. They cause a shift in your mind and an upheaval in your heart which can take time to forgive, heal, understand, and accept.

However, as you step into the season God has prepared for you – declare:

- I have what it takes.
- I am blessed and I cannot be cursed.
- I am the head and not the tail.
- I am blessed in the city and blessed in the field.
- I will make it no matter how I feel.
- I walk by faith not by sight.
- I am an overcomer.
- I am a winner.
- I am healed.
- I have the favour of God.
- I am fearfully and wonderfully made by God.
- I've got courage, strength, stamina, and ability to make it; for God is on my side.
- I shall not die, but live, to declare the glory of God in my life.

May these words comfort the mother whose child is in jail, on drugs, or in rebellion. May it comfort the wife who feels that it is impossible to live with an insensitive husband. May it bring healing and restoration to broken hearts, and damaged relationships. Starting today, have a good opinion of who you are. If you will get into the habit of speaking positive empowering affirming thoughts, you will not only have more confidence, but a wonderful, productive, spirit-filled, and successful life.

- Take a few minutes of silence to reflect over your life. What are your dreams for the future? What has held you back from pursuing your destiny?

Its Time to Shift Gears!

Prayer this Psalm 5: 2-10

Have mercy upon me O Lord, for I am weak. O Lord heal me for my bones are vexed. My soul is also sore vexed, but thou O Lord how long? Return O Lord, deliver my soul. O save for thy mercies sake. For in death there is no remembrance of thee, in the grave who shall give thee thanks? I am weary with my groaning, all the night make I my bed to swim, I water my couch with my tears. Mine eye is consumed because of grief; it waxeth old because of all mine enemies. Depart from me all ye workers of iniquity, for the Lord hath heard the voice of my weeping. The Lord hath heard my supplication; the Lord will receive my prayer. Let my mine enemies be ashamed and sore vexed, let them return and be ashamed suddenly.

Meditate on these Promises:

- *I shall be like a tree planted by the rivers of water, that bringeth forth fruit in my season, my leaves shall not wither, and whatsoever I do shall prosper.* Psalms 1:3

- *I cried unto the Lord with my voice, and he heard me out of his holy hill. I laid me down and slept, I awaked for the Lord sustained me. I will not be afraid of ten thousands of people that have set themselves against me round about.* Psalms 3: 4-6

- *The Lord had set apart him that is godly for himself; the Lord will hear when I call unto him.* Psalms 4:3

- *I will bless the Lord who hath given me counsel; my reins also instruct me in the night seasons. I have set the Lord always before me, because he is at my right hand, I shall not be moved.* Psalms 16:7-8

- *I will love thee, O Lord my strength. The Lord is my rock and my fortress, and my deliverer, my God, my strength, in whom I will trust; my buckler, and the horn of my salvation, and my high tower. I will call upon the Lord who is worthy to be praised, so shall I be saved from my enemies.* Psalms 18: 1-3

- *For by thee I have run through a troop; and by my God have I leaped over a wall. As for God, his way is perfect, the word of the Lord is tried, he is a buckler to all those that trust in him. It is God that girdeth me with strength, and maketh my way perfect.* Psalms 18: 29, 30, 32

Soul Searching & Inventory Exercise

Speak Life & Embrace Change

On the basis of fulfilling your purpose, all adversity works together for our good and God's glory. It is important to take the time needed to evaluate your situation and ask God to give you the wisdom and trust Him to give you the help you need. For this chapter's exercise, answer the following questions and develop your personal affirmations for the identified situations.

Part One

Write down 5 words to describe how you feel right now?

_____

_____

_____

_____

_____

What do you do to combat negativity and reassure yourself of how amazing you are?

_____

_____

_____

_____

_____

When I think about letting go what fears come up?

_____

_____

_____

_____

_____

What are you learning about yourself during this season of your life?

_____

_____

_____

_____

_____

What are the words you've been waiting to hear from someone you trust?

_____

_____

_____

_____

_____

_____

_____

Part Two

At some point, or the other, everyone needs affirmations. Life can be challenging, but affirmations serve as a reminder of how great we are and how we can depend on God to see us through. Draft your personal affirmations by completing the following phrases:

I'm thankful for

_____

_____

_____

_____

_____

I'm proud of

_____

_____

_____

_____

_____

_____

I feel supported when

_____

_____

_____

_____

_____

I feel inspired when

_____

_____

_____

_____

_____

I can achieve my goals because

_____

_____

_____

_____

_____

_____

I am valuable and

_____

_____

_____

_____

I love myself for who I am because

_____

_____

_____

_____

_____

Dear God,

Almighty God I come to you in the Name of Jesus asking you for wisdom, knowledge, and understanding.

Give me the strength and the ability to control my thoughts and my actions.

Help me to think on things that are true, honorable, just, pure, lovely, and of a good report.

May the words of my mouth, and the meditation of my heart, be acceptable in your sight for you are my strength and my Redeemer.

I take authority over every negative thought and over the negative voices that seeks to overwhelm my mind.

I dismantle, cancel, and disapprove it right now in the Name of Jesus.

Thank you for your healing power over my life – in Jesus Name Amen.

4
Chapter

Deal With It!

Let all bitterness, and wrath, and anger and clamour,
and evil speaking be put away from you, with all malice.
And be ye kind one to another, tenderhearted, forgiving
one another, even as God for Christ's sake hath forgiven you.
Ephesians 4:31-32

No matter what situation you find yourself in, when things do not turn out the way you think they should or the way you want them to, there comes a time when you got to deal with it! When vexation, regret, and sometimes remorsefulness takes mastery of your emotions, these events cause shifts in our minds and pandemonium in our hearts. This is no time to sulk in those feelings, on the contrary, this is the time we need to get to the root cause of the problem.

During your most laborious challenge or distressing experience, it is not the pain, shame, or guilt which will "haunt" you; it is your attempt to run away from it. When you run away from your challenges, you stunt your ability to grow. Instead of running from your fears, you must deal with it. Your growth is your business, and it has nothing to do with how anyone else is growing. The time spent watching and comparing yourself to others is the time that you should be spending to develop your skills to heighten your future. Stop wasting time worrying about other people's chapters and focus on your own. We ALL have a story to tell, and every story is unique. While you spend your days worrying about someone else's story you're missing out on developing your main character – you!

As you reflect over your life, you may feel that the succession of incidents you have encountered made it grim to believe you even have purpose. Even though it is hard to believe, I need for you to know that you do have a purpose. Jeremiah 29:11 reminds us, *For I know the thoughts that I think toward you saith the Lord, thoughts of peace and not of evil, to give you an expected end.*

Many of us at some time, or another, have experienced hurt; or in some instances, have caused hurt to someone. However, during this time we never really take the time to look inside to get honest and real with ourselves. Instead, we simply deal with the surface issues. We fail to get to the root of the problem and simply resort to striking back and hurting others. As we all know there is the saying, "Hurt people, hurt people." When you walk around with a lot of unresolved anger, you tend to attract angry situations, and hostile people. When you walk around feeling positive, and self-assured, you bring out the best in others and create harmony around you. It's time to deal with the effects of your failed relationships or failed business ventures; it's time to move on!

God does not want you to be in pain. However, He will not interfere with the choices you make. If you choose to stay in an abusive relationship, an unfulfilling job, a chaotic family environment, or any other harmful situation, God will not interfere! He will not move you until you are ready to be moved. You may have convinced yourself that you have done too much hideous things for God to still be with you. Nothing can be further from the truth. God is a merciful God. He is your present help in time of trouble.

Very often we blame God for what has happened to us. We get angry because things did not go the way we want them to go. In the long run, we abandon God by resigning ourselves to pain and suffering. My dear readers, no matter what has happened, where you have been, or what you have done, you cannot move beyond pain, fear, and disappointment until you deal with your messed up ideologies. Until you have come to the realization that life, without God, makes no sense!

For lasting, positive change, you must go deeper and not merely look at what you do; but ask yourself, "What is the root problem?" Why do I act this way?" Why am I out of control in this area?" "Why do I feel that I must repeatedly prove myself to everybody?" It is only until you get to the root and start dealing with the source of the problem that you can realistically expect positive change. You need to examine carefully the areas in which you constantly struggle. Is your partner really at fault? Is it really your circumstances, upbringing, or environment? Or could it be that you have something buried deep within that is causing you to be the way you are.

Many of us have had similar experiences in our lives. Somebody did us wrong, and rather than letting it go, we chose to hold on to it. Know this, bitterness contaminates every part of your being, and creates additional stress. In addition, there are times when you cannot seem to get along with a particular person, and you become certain that it must be their fault. Is it possible that the problem could be you? Could it be that you have a root of pride that is causing you to withhold forgiveness? You must deal with the core issue, or else the problem will keep coming back until you get to the real source.

It is only when we choose to try to change that we see positive results. What is your decision? What are you afraid of? Are you choosing to become bitter, or allowing the situation to make you into a better person? According to psychologist Dennis O'Grady, the ability to change is related to a combination of five fears that can choke one's ability to change:

1. **Fear of the Unknown** - The unspoken message from society says that when change occurs, you will lose control.

2. **Fear of Failure** - If I commit myself to goals for change, there is a chance for failure.

3. **Fear of Commitment** - Commitment forces an answer to tough questions. "What do I really want?" Commitment to one option is not always fun because it eliminates other options.

4. **Fear of Disapproval** - If I change, I risk having people say they liked me better the way I was. Your own change also forces others to change in relationship to you.

5. **Fear of Success** - If I change what other demands will be made of me? Can I sustain this success?

Right now, you may be plagued with the memories of your past. Your present situation, and the pressure to make the right choice may be weighing heavily on your mind. Today, you can break free from anything that has held you back; however, you have to make a conscious effort to do your part. Be honest and face the truth about yourself. You may be facing a seemingly desperate situation right now; you may have come out of an abusive situation. Maybe the people who raised you were unkind, or somebody with whom you shared a relationship used you, abused you, and now you are dealing with the ramifications of that bad relationship.

Please, do not let that be an excuse for you to refuse to give yourself a chance to live, and love, again. You have worth and value. Desperately cling to life; not only for yourself, but for those whom you are to be a blessing to. Sometimes life's adversities intimidate us and put added stress on us that ultimately terminate our dreams and visions. Though the vision tarries, you must wait for it! It will come to pass! I speak prophetically over your life, "If you are in a state of passiveness, dryness, coldness, and half-heartedness, I dare you to RISE UP from where you are. You are coming out! You will accomplish the will of God for your life! No longer will you be dominated by circumstances; instead, you will take command over anything, or anyone designated to nullify, delay, curtail, or bring to an untimely end the plan of God for your life."

Several years ago, I went through a very painful time in my life, as I misjudged certain situations and made what I consider to be serious mistakes. The more I understood the choices I had made, the worse I felt about myself. "How could I have allowed this to happen to me?" "How stupid am I?" I lamented. "After all my hard work and investment, I should have been much more vigilant, more observant, and more attentive. It was in this season of disapproval of my life I decided to do a bit of reflection.

I can vividly remember it was the year I was just about to graduate from high school. My menstrual cycle was immature. There were no physical signs that I was pregnant, until one morning my reflection surprised me. After several pregnancy tests and a trip to see the doctor, I found out that I was six weeks pregnant. Petrified and not certain how to break the news to my parents, my days of guilt and contemplation were outnumbered as the thoughts of abortion, eloping, or facing my worst nightmare of the reproach from society and the church overwhelmed me. Dreams of college dissipated. I was ashamed and had become a disappointment to my parents and myself. I was depressed and finally opted to elope; and eventually after much highs and lows, our family was restored. Years later, I attended college and graduated with honors. Upon my return from college, I worked at the Department of Social Services where I mentored adolescent mothers. God restored my broken years, and gave me the magic of motherhood. Seeing my daughter Keyler's accomplishments is a true reflection of God's goodness is my life.

So how are you going to handle your dilemma? How will you choose to respond? You may have been here before, in this, or a similar situation. As you travel through this journey life, roadblocks come and go, but the truth remains constant. Our lessons are unavoidable. Are you going to run, or hide? Are you going to pout, or create drama? The choice is yours, but remember life is watching you. God is watching you. Don't fail the test! Deal with it!

My prayer for you during this season of change is that God will empower you to see further beyond your present situation. I encourage you, amidst what you are up against *Deal with It*! Find your strength in God. Refuse to let your future die right before your very eyes. I was able to draw from the strength of God – you can too! My confidence was in knowing that *I can do all things through Christ which strengthens me.* (Philippians 4:13). My assurance came from knowing that *He who had begun this work within me would be faithful to complete it even until the day of Jesus Christ.* (Philippians 1:6)

I am taking a Stand for me!

HERE ARE SOME QUESTIONS YOU CAN ASK YOURSELF WHEN FACED WITH OBSTACLES:

1. How can I use this to grow?

2. How well am I dealing with this situation?

3. What is life teaching me in this lesson?

4. What is God trying to teach me?

SCRIPTURES TO GET YOU THROUGH TOUGH TIMES:

- *"Search me, O God, and know my heart, try me and know my thoughts. See if there be any wicked way in me and lead me in the way everlasting."* Psalm 139:23-24

- *"Casting all your care upon him for he careth for you."* 1 Peter 5:7

- *"If I regard iniquity in my heart, the Lord will not hear me."* Psalm 66:18

- *"The Lord also will be a refuge for the oppressed a refuge in times of trouble."* Psalms 9:9-10

- *"Restore unto me the joy of thy salvation; and uphold me with thy free spirit."* Psalms 51:12

- *Fret not thyself because of evildoers, neither be thou envious against the workers of iniquity.....* Psalms 37:1-40

Soul Searching & Inventory Exercise

Deal With It!

Expressing and exercising your faith can lead to you becoming fully whole and healed. Journal your thoughts and emotions so that you can be transformed in a positive way.

What anger or frustration are you still holding onto?

_____

_____

_____

_____

_____

_____

Why have you held on to it for so long?

_____

_____

_____

_____

_____

_____

What has resulted from you holding on to your anger or frustration?

_____

_____

_____

_____

_____

_____

Who do you need to forgive?

_____

_____

_____

_____

_____

Why is it important to forgive?

_____

_____

_____

_____

_____

DEAL WITH IT!

What are some things that you like about yourself that others seem to criticize you about?

_____

_____

_____

_____

_____

Are you upset with God about something that has taken place in your life?

_____

_____

_____

_____

_____

Why do you blame God for this?

_____

_____

_____

_____

_____

What story or justification have you been telling yourself that no longer serves you?

_____

_____

_____

_____

_____

How can you use your hurt and pain to change situations/or help someone else?

_____

_____

_____

_____

_____

Dear God,

Sovereign Lord, I come to you today in the name of Jesus.
I ask of you to heal me from my brokenness.

Heal me from resentment, anger, and bitterness.
God of mercy and grace, when I am surrounded by the memories
of my past, surround me with your presence and unfailing love.

When I feel hurt and angry, due to unmet expectations, help me
to be reminded that my satisfaction comes from only you.

May your word refresh my spirit, renew my soul, and empower me
to be more like you. Through Jesus Christ our Lord Amen.

5

Chapter

I am Coming Out Of This!

"After Nathan had gone home, the LORD struck the child that Uriah's wife had borne to David, and he became ill. David pleaded with God for the child. He fasted and spent the nights lying in sackcloth on the ground. The elders of his household stood beside him to get him up from the ground, but he refused, and he would not eat any food with them. On the seventh day the child died. David's attendants were afraid to tell him that the child was dead, for they thought, "While the child was still living, he wouldn't listen to us when we spoke to him. How can we now tell him the child is dead? He may do something desperate." David noticed that his attendants were whispering among themselves, and he realized the child was dead. "Is the child dead?" he asked. "Yes," they replied, "he is dead." Then David got up from the ground. Washed and anointed himself and changed his clothes, and he went into the house of the LORD and worshiped. Then he went to his own house, and at his request they served him food, and he ate. His attendants asked him, "Why are you acting this way? While the child was alive, you fasted and wept, but now that the child is dead, you get up and eat!"
2 Samuel 12" 15-21

We have caught David at a crossroad in his life. Under David's rule, the Lord caused many nations to prosper. He was anointed to be king over Israel. He was anointed with grace and power to do exploits for the Kingdom of God. David was the one who had been mighty in battle. He overthrew the Philistines, causing them to become helpless repeatedly. He was the one who ruined Goliath's reputation as being big and bad. He killed Goliath with a stone and a sling and walked away; a little boy carrying a big man's head.

Despite all his successes, we see from the Word of God where he had some weaknesses and some failures. He had some character flaws. He made bad choices. He fell in love with somebody else's wife and wanted her so bad that he impregnated her and had her husband killed to keep her!

Later, we found David praying after he had received word from Nathan that God had pronounced death over the child. It is easy to see that at that moment, David was at a real low point in his life. He cried out to God asking Him to fix it! He begged God to save his child's life.

In this life, there are times when we tell ourselves we have got it all together, that we have things under control. Well, I have come by to tell you that regardless of the control that you think you have over your life, God wants you to know that He is your Creator and that He is in total control of your life.

It is a difficult task when you are trying to save something that God is trying to get rid of. Like David, you might be struggling and fighting with some issues in your life that God wants to abolish. However, what do you do when you are asking God for something that's going this way, and God's answer is going the other way? David was good at fighting external fights. Give him a giant, and he will kill it. Give him an army, and he will destroy them. But may I ask! What do you do when your greatest enemy is not out there? What do you do when your greatest enemy is on the inside?

I hear you saying, "I do not want to go through this. I cannot take it any longer. It is too much for me to handle." I hear you saying, "God, I know that you are a healer, but if receiving your healing means I have to be sick, I do not want it. I know that you are a way maker, but if I have to be in a position where my back is against the wall in order to witness the miracle, I don't think I can do that. Lord, I know that you are a provider, but if I have to be broke as a joke in order to see you make a way out of no way, I don't think I'm okay with that. I want to have a great testimony and a strong anointing like the people I see in the front line, but I do not want to go through the mess they went through. I want it, but I just do not want the suffering and the pain that comes with it."

Listen, for you to experience the supernatural power of God in your life, you cannot resist going through difficult moments. However, he knows the way that you take! This means you must have the utmost confidence in Him. Though you cannot see Him, He sees you, and He knows what's in your heart. No matter what people may say, or however they may misunderstand your character, God knows the inner most parts of you. Therefore, you must have the fullest confidence that He will bring you through.

Though your life may be rough, God wants you to rely on His providence. As you ponder over your life, you may have had some near-death experiences. There were times when you probably told yourself you were a "bad mamma jamma". You may have felt you could contend with anything or anyone who opposed you. You see, this fight David fought was not physical. It was a fight for his life! David was at a point of desperation, fighting for a life he almost destroyed with the mess he created! And just like so many of you, this battle was taking place in his mind.

Listen to me, it is not about your haters, it is not about the money you have, it is not about your enemies, nor is it about what they say about you… No! The battle ground is in your mind!"

Joyce Meyer, in her book, *Start your New Life Today states*, "If we want to see God's perfect will proven in our lives – we can – but our minds must be transformed. We have to think different thoughts and look at life differently. We must begin to think in agreement with God's Word and not the devil's lies." (p.77)

Romans 12-2 emphasizes, *Be not conformed to this world, but be ye transformed by the renewing of you mind.* The time has come for you to stop wasting your weapons on what people say about you. You see, it is not what they say about you that matters. It is what God says about you. It is what you say about you that threatens your destiny!

Think about this, for seven days David did not eat. Imagine being in such a position! As a matter of fact, I know that some of you have experienced going through a rough time in your life, and everyone seems to have a front row seat to your demise. Nothing they do, or say, seems to make any sense. Delayed does not mean denied. It may in fact mean that the blessing coming is so much bigger than the one you lost, and it will be worth the wait, and worth the prayer to see the vision come to fruition.

Can you relate to this dilemma? Have you ever wanted something so badly that you would do anything to attain it? Perhaps it was money that you desired after growing up in hard times. Or maybe it was a leadership position. Or was it that young man or woman that you loved dearly? If you have been through a loss, or one of your dreams has died, there's a time for you to wallow in your grief; but at some point you need to pick yourself up, dust yourself off, put on a fresh attitude, and start moving forward in life.

God's promise for us is so much more, so much bigger than we could ever imagine. We must trust that God knows how far to take us and let Him carry us to that place. As you prepare to come out of your dilemma. You must be ready and able to combat fear, overcome procrastination, and be free from your failures. It is about you being willing, ready, and able to dispose your past. *Forgetting those things which are behind and reaching forth unto those things which are before.* (Philippians 3:13).

I speak prophetically over your life. Now is the time to step into ***your*** divine ***destiny***! You have too much to lose to allow whatever you are facing to destroy you. I dare you to throw it behind you:

- ✔ Every Doubt
- ✔ Every Fear
- ✔ Every Worry
- ✔ Every Anxiety
- ✔ Every Negative situation that has kept you back
- ✔ Everything that kept you up at nights.

Regardless of all the natural evidence, despite the stench of death in the face of your childhood insecurities; notwithstanding all odds being against you when everybody around expects you to give up and die… I decree and declare a sudden change over your life and over your circumstances.

- They say you are never going to make it.
- They say that you will never get up.
- They say that you will never go on with your life.
- They say that you will never amount to anything good.

No matter how impossible your dreams may seem, you continue to hope. No matter how upset you become when you look around and see fewer deserving people with what your heart was built for, don't give up. Yes, you may have days when it feels like your hope has sunk. You will have moments when you cannot muster enough hope to move a mustard seed. However, that's when you got to find your strength in God. The Lord has brought you this far, protected you, nurtured you, and placed dreams inside you. I challenge you to allow your faith to reach beyond the many breaches in life and climb up walls of impossibility.

Follow Your Dreams!

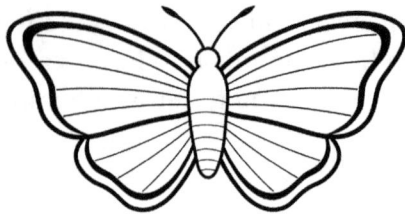

MEDITATION SCRIPTURES

✔ *I can do all things through Christ which strengtheneth me.*
Philippians 4:13

✔ *Be strong and of a good courage, fear not, nor be afraid of them: for the LORD thy God, it is he that doth go with thee; he will not fail thee, nor forsake thee.* Deuteronomy 31:6

✔ *For the LORD your God is he that goeth with you, to fight for you against your enemies, to save you.* Deuteronomy 20:4

✔ *There hath no temptation taken you but such as is common to man: but God is faithful, who will not suffer you to be tempted above that ye are able; but will with the temptation also make a way to escape, that ye may be able to bear it.*
1 Corinthians 10:13

✔ *Come unto me, all ye that labour and are heavy laden, and I will give you rest.* Matthew 11:28

Soul Searching & Inventory Exercise

I'm Coming Out Of This!

Each of the following questions are designed to support you in healing and releasing non-productive thoughts, feelings, and behaviors. The key is to answer every question as honestly as you possibly can.

1. As a result of this experience, I learned...

_____

_____

_____

_____

_____

_____

2. This made me feel…

_____

_____

_____

_____

_____

_____

3. How do I want others to see me?

_____

_____

_____

_____

_____

_____

4. What is my most perceived weakness?

_____

_____

_____

_____

_____

5. How can I turn it into a strength?

_____

_____

_____

_____

_____

6. What are some of the things I need to let go of to fulfil my purpose in life?

_____

_____

_____

_____

_____

Dear God,

I come to you in the Name of Jesus. Please give me the strength to endure this situation that I am faced with.

Guide my thoughts, my words, and my actions. Remove the darkness from my life and fill me with the light of your truth.

Give me the strength to overcome temptation and fleshy desires. I believe that you are more than able to keep that which I commit to you.

Forgive me of all my sins and renew a right spirit within. I surrender my life to you.

Use me for your honor and your glory. I give you praise and thanks for this. In Jesus Name Amen.

6

Chapter

A Message In The Mess!

*A happy heart makes the face cheerful, but heartache
crushes the spirit.*
Proverbs 15:13

As you go through life, you will understand that you must go through things – whether good or bad. Some of you may not have had the support of others to get you through the pit experiences, and this may cause you to feel down and out! The circumstances that have surrounded your life, and the series of hurt that you have endured over the years, has made you to feel like a nobody. It has probably made you feel ostracized, forsaken, and like the black sheep in the family. Right now, you may be at a point in your life where you are about to throw in the towel. I speak life into your dead situation.

Some of you literally beat yourself up by listening to the negative voice within telling you, "You blew it. You messed up. There's no hope for you." Instead of believing that you are growing and improving, you believe the voice that's telling you that you cannot do anything right. You will never break this habit, and you are just a failure. As a result, you become extremely critical of yourself.

The time has come for you to regroup, refocus, and build spiritual strength and stamina to step over the setbacks you face in life; because whilst there is life, there is hope.

There was a time when I felt guilty over the mistakes I had made in my life. Little did I know, it was preparing me for my due season. You may be challenged by the many problems that distress you. Never allow your circumstances to be an impediment to you succeeding in life. Despite the naysayers and the critics, amidst the ridicule and condemnation, I kept the faith and relied totally on God. Today, I give God praise and thanks for enabling me to fulfill my purpose.

I am of the firm belief that irrespective of your bad experiences in life, they can create favourable circumstances if you change your thought pattern. This statement draws me back to a time in my life when I held on to the thought that I must live to please everyone. Imagine that! My life was like a roller coaster – up today, down tomorrow, tearful moments, and gloomy days. I grew frustrated, miserable, bitter, and most of all unfulfilled. After much deliberation with myself, I had no other choice but to decide once and for all to do what was best for me.

Sometimes we need to take the blame and responsibility for where we are positioned in life. I use to cast blame on all kinds of outside forces. Parents, people, relationships, children, fate…. I never really stopped to think that I was the major contributor to the things that were taking place in my life. I was the common denominator in every trial and setback I'd endured. A few years ago, I experienced what seemed to be a mass of insoluble problems in my life. Year after year I watched my life being eaten away. Daily I watched myself slip into a state of depression. I felt hopeless. For years I had robbed myself from experiencing true happiness. Why do I always have to learn the hard way? This was a question I frequently asked myself. It was in these times I learned that happiness is a choice. That was one of the greatest gifts I'd ever given myself – learning to love me!

Today, when presented with opposition, I know it is up to me to find the good and to be happy regardless of what is happening around me. I no longer point fingers, or play the blame game. I know that it is up to me to choose how I will respond; knowing that I am in control of my happiness, and no one can take that away from me. It is necessary for you to understand that to master the art of finding happiness you need to rid your life of negativity.

As you go forth in discovering your true happiness, learn to focus on positive things. It does not matter how devastating the situation might seem, you can learn from your bad experiences. There is a message in your mess. You might be hurting right now, but you just might not understand everything that is going on in your life. Understand this, God never wastes a hurt. The Bible says, "He comforts us in all our troubles, so that we can comfort others" If you really desire to be used by God, you must understand this powerful truth. The very experiences that you have resented, or regretted, most in your life are the experiences God wants to use to help others. They are your ministry!

It is time for you to do a bit of introspection. The time has come for you to remove the mask. Most of the times we wear a painted smile, when deep inside we are hurting. Are you ready to remove the veil? It is time to honestly admit your faults, your failures, your fears, and your hurts. Why not close your eyes and mediate on some of the things that have held you back from achieving your goals… that restrict you from functioning effectively?

Is it your relationship, children, husband, wife, work, money, or your health? Whatever the obstacles, know this that God is in control. You can, and will, win the battle over whatever situation confronts you. What I have learned, over the years, is that at times we think that the problems we face in life are sent to destroy us. The Bible made it emphatically clear that *All things work together for our good.* (Romans 8:28) If you would only take the time to examine the situation, you will see the opportunity and lessons to be learned in every challenge you face.

In the midst of what seems chaotic, take the pressure off yourself; give yourself the right to have some weaknesses and trust God to work your situation out for you. Quit listening to the accusing voice. Quit going around feeling sorry for yourself. Summon the strength, courage, and confidence of the phenomenal woman that you are. You've got to resist the urge to quit, squander, weep without hope, and resign yourself to destroy your destiny. From today forward, all things are made new!

As you read this book, and you reflect over your life, you may experience flashbacks of the mental damage of excuses such as *It's too late. You'll never find your place. You are too old, too tired, too uneducated, too poor.* All of these are excuses standing in the way of exercising faith in action. Excuses are lies of the enemy binding you to the past. It's time to release yourself from excuses and magnify what the Lord has planted in you – GREATNESS!

Today is the day of new beginnings. Speak life not death in the mess!

- ✔ I am blessed
- ✔ I am coming out of this
- ✔ I am beautiful
- ✔ I am valuable
- ✔ I am qualified
- ✔ I am equipped
- ✔ I am empowered
- ✔ I am fearfully and wonderfully made by God.

When you get through this mess, you are going to be much better off. You will have a new assessment of your strength and greater insights about the people in your life. In the midst of the challenge, your eyes will be opened, your mind will be exposed to new levels of awareness, and your spiritual life will be heightened. When you get through this, you are going to be something else; a better, stronger you!

I Really am okay With Me!!

PRINCIPLES TO APPLY TO YOUR DAILY LIFE:

- Happiness is a decision I make; it is not given to me by anyone.
- Nothing can make me unhappy without my permission.
- I will think positively, and adapt a positive attitude.
- I will love and accept myself.
- I will be nice to other people no matter what.
- I will believe in myself.
- I will choose to be positive.
- I will get rid of negative thoughts.

Soul Searching & Inventory Exercise

A Mess In The Message

It's time to delve deeper into your past hurts and current frustrations. This exercise is designed to narrow down areas that you must overcome. Growth is always necessary.

Part One

What characteristics in your life indicate that you haven't fully forgiven your past hurts?

_____

_____

_____

_____

_____

I no longer want to feel angry and frustrated; I would love to feel…

_____

_____

_____

_____

_____

I no longer blame myself for these problems…

_____

_____

_____

_____

_____

In order to focus on fulfilling my purpose, I need to…

_____

_____

_____

_____

I am stronger than I used to be. Here's why…

_____

_____

_____

_____

_____

_____

A MESSAGE IN THE MESS!

Part Two

Take a moment to write a letter to yourself, regarding self-forgiveness, for the mistakes you've made in the past.

_____

_____

_____

_____

_____

_____

_____

_____

_____

_____

_____

_____

_____

Dear God,

Heavenly Father, I come to you today, in the name of Jesus. I need hope for a better future.

I need hope for a better life. I am frustrated and tired with my present position.

Almighty God, I need your help. Give me the strength, oh God, to overcome these negative feelings.

I pray that you bless me and fill me with happiness and peace of mind.

Grant me your supernatural wisdom and guidance in everything I do, so that my words and actions will honor your Holy Name. In Jesus' Name I pray – Amen

Chapter

Your Strength Is In Your Struggle

"We are hard-pressed on every side, yet not crushed, we are perplexed, but not in despair, persecuted but not forsaken, struck down but not destroyed."
2 Corinthians 4: 8-9

Many of our troubles in life occur because we base our choices on the notion that "everyone is doing it". We allude to the famous saying, "If it feels right – just do it!" What is important is that you need to develop a set standard that will never lead you in the wrong direction. The most important decision you can make is to decide that regardless of what is taking place around you – whether cultural, traditional, or emotional, you choose only that which is right.

Just think about your life for a moment. How did you learn your most valuable lesson? I remember attending a Motivational Seminar, and the topic of how each of us face challenges in life was discussed. Many of the couples shared their varied experiences. There was a particular young lady who was overwhelmed to tears as she described the insurmountable problems she faced from her abusive husband. My own face was wet with tears as I listened to her tell her truth to a room of complete strangers. What was outstanding about her is, though she felt abused and ostracized, though she felt worthless and insignificant, at the end of her sharing, she smiled and thanked God for what she had been through.

Have you ever taken the time to thank God for the problems you have experienced in life? Have you ever taken the time to honor your obstacles in life? Most of you might be saying, "You've got to be crazy! After all I've been through you are talking about honoring? Sonia, I can see myself accepting and learning from my mistakes, but honoring, I cannot digest that! How can I honor something that made me so miserable? I just don't believe I can do that!" And to that, I say, "Yes you can!"

I need you to understand that problems have a purpose. They have something specific to offer you; and just for the record, the longer you take to receive the message, the longer they will stick around! This is food for thought, which can be motivating as well; if there are lessons to be learned from your obstacles, do you want to take four years to learn them, or four days? Do you want to wrestle and resist, or do you want to work towards getting the message quickly so you can move on?

Have you noticed that when faced with a problem, if you do not deal with it in the right way, it remains with you until you do? That is what I am talking about. If you choose to ignore, or retaliate, until you have dealt with the matter in its entirety, you will become enslaved. Problems are there to make us grow and learn. I am of the firm belief that God prepares us for greater opportunities, only if we are willing to let go and let God.

You cannot afford to go through life like a leaf in the wind. It is about learning to trust God and His timing in your life. What we need to understand is that our timing is not God's timing. If you would look at your life and the mistakes that you have made, I am sure that regrettably you can say, "I messed up here. Back in the days I was so rebellious. If I had only known, I should have waited." Time and time again you have heard that still small voice ministering to you by means of the Holy

Spirit, and yet you chose to resist, you chose to be stiff-necked, and it caused you to live with regret.

The time has come for you to pick yourself up and let your faith take you somewhere you have never been. Yes! The time has come for you to step out of the shadows of your life. Jesus made it emphatically clear in the book of Proverbs 24:16, *A just man falleth seven times and riseth up again.* There's no need for you to pretend to be someone you are not. It's sad that often it takes a crisis, or tragedy, to jolt us into an awareness of our lives and the way we live. What's sadder is when people come to the surface after such an event and are not willing to risk pursuing their dreams when given a second and a third chance. You don't have to wait until catastrophe strikes to count the cost of what you are living for! Why not take an inventory of your life, today!

My dear readers, I hope to challenge you to make your life be one of excellence. I beseech you to fan the flame of life and hope; desiring more out of life, knowing that when God created you, He had greatness in mind. For too long you have wrestled with the cares of life. Yes! You have been labeled so many times by your critics that you have lost your joy and enthusiasm for living. I empathize with you; I have been there, but you must not allow it to control your life. You are more than a conqueror through Christ!

If you are reading this book, you have likely experienced a desire to change. I urge you to build your life on a foundation of prayer. For you to be victorious, prayers must not be secondary, but primary. Gone are the days for casual prayers. It is all about warfare intercession. What you must understand is that your warfare is not of the devil. It is because the Lord is purifying the body… He is purifying your ministry. He is also shaping your character- and anything that can be shaken in the process will be shaken until purification takes place.

Too often we try to take matters into our own hands. We do whatever we feel is best to make it to the top – even if it means stepping on others. Our society tells us to "fake it till we make it." I am here to tell you that it takes much more courage to share who you really are, but God is willing to take your sad story and give you a glory experience. He will give you beauty for ashes and strength for your pain.

As you are developed by the brutal realities of life that have tarnished your reputation, character and integrity know this; there is no need for you to worry about the life you once lived. God has got that under cover. Many of us, when faced with adversity, what do we do? We tend to worry! God says, *Be anxious for nothing, but in everything by prayer and supplication, with thanksgiving, let your requests be made known to God.* (Philippians 4:6). The time has come for you to position yourself for the new thing He is about to do in your life. However, this will not be an automatic process. It is about working in His timing.

Learning to wait on God is critical. For some of you, I believe the patience you have to exhibit in waiting can become frustrating and time consuming. However, it is crucial for your success. It is in waiting you will be refined and re-designed. God will mold and craft you into the person He wants you to be.

I challenge you to examine your life. Ask yourself: Who do I fear most? Whose power do I respect most? The power of God? Or the power of my enemies? I implore you to look beyond the image you see in the mirror, and see the person you were created to be. Dare to put your faith, trust, and confidence in the God of the impossible, who said that, *He will never leave you nor forsake you.*

What is God calling you to do today? What must you let go of in order for Him to have first place in your life? Well, let me tell you, it might cost you losing friends and family. You most definitely will have to give up your personal agenda – dying to self and allowing God's will to permeate and supersede your fleshy desires. However, let me warn you that the cost of greatness does not come easily.

As I climbed the ladder of success, with its many demands, I can tell you it was not easy. There were times when I felt like giving up due to incessant negative accusations hurled against me. There were times when I had to pause for a moment along the way to literally energize myself from the mouths of people. There were times when I even felt inadequate, ill-equipped, and terrified. There were times when I felt like giving up, but something always brought me back on track. Despite the setbacks, I had to remain focused. I had to stay on course. It took a lot of hard work, perseverance and sacrifice to be where I am today.

The influential story of Martin Luther King Junior and his attempt to change the face of history has always inspired me. His famous speech, "I Have a Dream," is known worldwide, and because of his sacrifices (and the sacrifices of many other civil rights leaders like him), black people are now using the same washroom, eating in the same restaurants, and sitting in the same seats as white people. He did all this because he dared to dream. I want to tell you, my dear readers, that as you take another step in life's journey, you need to dream. Dream big dreams that would make you into a better person. I believe Mr. King must have felt like throwing in the towel at some point, but he withstood the test of time.

What about Sonia Whitlock, Mother Teresa, Oprah Winfrey, Billy Graham, and Wilton Nancis? Never assume that it was easy for these empowered people who have blessed our world by stepping into their destiny. It does not matter what you have been called to in this life, I encourage you to aspire to be great. Leave a legacy behind for your children and grandchildren. In life, it is only the strong who will survive! It takes a big person, with a big character and big dreams to make big things happen, and that person is you!

Many people are born with an unconscious expectation that they are supposed to come into this world already put together; already competent at living and loving. There comes a time in each of our lives when we must come to terms with the fact that the purpose of life is for you to grow into the best human being you can be. We don't come into this world having all the answers and we don't leave this world being anywhere close to having all the answers either.

So what is the purpose of your life? What value do you place on your life? Are you a quitter, or a fighter? Do you know that one of the most dangerous things in life is wasting time? When you discover your purpose, it gives you an epiphany to stop wasting your life, and then it challenges you to start fulfilling your potential.

However, even still, distractions are always there, and you must be careful not to become side-tracked along the way. There will be haters with evil intent, and you must guard yourself from them. Even still, I am of the firm belief that once you focus your time looking at the negative energy within yourselves in an effort to turn it into positive energy, your lives will be enhanced to one of fulfillment.

What I have observed is that half of the things we hate about others are qualities that can actually benefit us. During my lifetime, I have experienced and still am experiencing my share of criticism, but I have learned coping skills to deal with my opposers. I have learned to smile in the midst of adversity. Further, we hate what we do not understand. However, there is no need for the animosity. We all have different assignments to carry out in life. Only when we understand our uniqueness and purpose, would we be able to assist one another properly and fulfill the lives we were created to live. Do not let anybody fool you into believing that you are something that you are not. You should look inside to determine your design.

Rick Warren's book, "The Purpose Driven Life" outlined the benefits of living a purposeful life:

- ✔ Knowing your purpose gives life meaning.
- ✔ Knowing your purpose focuses your life.
- ✔ Knowing your purpose motivates your life.
- ✔ Knowing your purpose prepares you for eternity.
- ✔ Knowing your purpose simplifies life.

He further expressed, "Without a clear purpose you have no foundation on which to allocate your time and use your resources. Without this knowledge you tend to make choices based on circumstances, pressures, and your feelings."

This can be detrimental to your future. I urge you to start channeling your energies in knowing your purpose. Seek God to show you your life's course. God wants to use you in ways far beyond your wildest dreams. Like Abraham, Daniel, and Moses, we must have faith in God – believing that with Him nothing is impossible.

In light of this it is of utmost importance that you understand that there is no fulfillment in life without knowing your purpose. God created each of us with a purpose. That purpose is what is right for you. In order for you to find your true purpose, you need to seek God continuously, and be in constant communication with Him. This is the pattern you must follow. Why? Well, it is dangerous to live without God. See, if you do not know God, you will NEVER know your reason for existence; and if you do not know why you were born, you could live a completely defeated life.

My aim is not just to motivate you, but to admonish you that it is crucial that you succeed in all spheres of your life. With this in mind, I need for you to place special emphasis on you. It is vital that you love yourself. Make sure you allow God to lead you so that you can reflect Him with a positive self-image and a healthy sense of self-worth. You might be saying, "Sonia, why should I love myself after all I have been through? I do not have any reason since throughout my life all I have mainly heard is ridicule." I say to you today, the time has come for you to release your past and learn to love yourself. The answer you are searching for dwells in God.

You must face your obstacles head-on, devising creative ways and means to succeed. It is your time to soar. You must begin by separating yourself. It does not matter how badly you messed up, or how often; you are still worthy and acceptable to God. The past is the past. God is not concerned about your past. He is concerned about your future! Who you used to be, doesn't matter anymore; what matters is who is in control of your life. With this in mind, and with God directing your steps, there is no need for you to contend, compete, or compromise your values to win the approval of others.

When God called Esther, major adjustments had to be made to her life. In the same way, as we prepare to go to another level, God will purge us inwardly. He will detach us from the crowd and uproot us from our normal ways of living. For most of us, we might not understand, and even question it. However, know this, nothing in life comes easy. You were bought with a price.

Jesus, Himself, was faced with difficult situations. How did He respond? Well, in the Garden of Gethsemane, He yielded to the desire of His Father and responded, *Not my will, but thine will be done.* Luke 22:42. He shed His blood on Calvary's cross for your sins. What do you have to give? As you move forward, as you press towards fulfilling the call of God in your life, you will be tried and tested, but you will find the strength in your struggles.

Each season of your life will bring added responsibilities and experiences. The method by which you approach this new season will determine your success or failure. Quit comparing yourself to everyone around you and submitting yourself to do what they are doing. Be a success in your own eyes, regardless of what is taking place around you. It does not matter if you are a housewife, a mechanic, or a secretary. It does not matter if you are a worship leader, or an intercessor. You must set standards for yourself which others can emulate. Know this, your job, or role, does not determine who you are!

For you to master the art of successful living, you must first work with your inward feelings. You must deal with the war that is going on inside of you. Some people are bitter with themselves, they are unable to accept who they are. One of the worst things you can do is go through life being against yourself. This is a major problem today. Trust me when I say, if you do not have a healthy respect for who you are, and if you do not learn to accept your faults, you will never be able to properly love other people. I have counselled many couples who think their partner is the reason they cannot get along in their relationship, or they are sure that it is their co-worker's fault; but the fact is they have a war raging on the inside. They are upset because they have not broken a bad habit, and that eventually is transferred into their other relationships.

Self-acceptance has been a long process for me. It came in different areas of my life over a period of time. I cannot remember anyone really talking to me about the vital importance of accepting myself. In all of this, there were times when I felt very insecure and out of place. But after four years at college, I saw another aspect of self-acceptance. I had to accept the fact that I was different from others. I needed to let go of the feelings of frustration and accept my own uniqueness. It's time to thank God for you. Your shape, your size, your ways, your disposition, your education, your abilities, and your struggles.

What you need to understand here is that you cannot give away what you do not have. If you do not love yourself, you are not going to be able to love others. If you feel angry or insecure about yourself then that is all you will have to give. On the other hand, if you learn to accept yourself, you can give that love away and have healthy relationships. Once you capture this principle, you are on your way to a renewed life and a new perception of others.

Yes! Even as you continue to transform and grow you will still have some faults. You may have some things you wish you could change about yourself, however, be encouraged. No one is perfect! I encourage you today to release and quit being so hard on yourself! I encourage you to shake off the guilt, condemnation, inadequacies, and the sense that you cannot measure up; and start feeling good about who you are. No matter how many mistakes you have made in the past, or what sort of difficulties you struggle with right now, you have been destined to live in victory. You may not be all you want to be, but at least you can look back and say, "Thank You Jesus; I am not what I used to be."

HERE ARE SOME TIPS TO ASSIST YOU TO BECOME A BETTER PERSON

- **Stop the Criticism:** Refuse to criticize yourself. When you approve of yourself, your changes are positive.

- **Praise yourself:** Praise yourself as much as you can. Tell yourself how well you are doing with every little thing.

- **Take a good look at the people with whom you tend to surround yourself:** Try making at least one new friend who is on a higher level in life than you.

- **Watch what you say about yourself.** Keep a mental record of your day.

- **Identify your good characteristics.** Write them down. Look at what skills you might have, and work hard in developing a specific area of your life.

- **Be determined to rise above your present level.** Involve yourself with someone else's problems and help solve them.

- **Let go of yourself by releasing your feelings, whatever they may be, into God's hands.** Give the situation to Him through an effort of commitment.

- **Look into the mirror and speak positively into your life.** Express this growing sense of love you have for yourself. Forgive yourself looking into the mirror. At least once a day say: "I love you, I really love you!"

As you progress into a new season of your life, I say to all of you reading this book, the time has come to take off the mask! Stop doing the impersonations and take your center stage, fulfilling the role you were born to play. Some of you prefer to stay behind the mask, because you've allowed it to become a shield, protecting you from anyone getting too close. However, understand that is not a part of the whole armor of God, and it is in fact a counterfeit! I understand, you have experienced so much hardship and anguish in life so you wear your mask as a defense, a façade that doesn't reveal your vulnerability and your weakness. Beloved, do not forfeit who you are, in pursuit of playing a role that was not designed for you. Be true to your character; boldly TAKE THE LIMITS OFF of your life and claim your place in the world! Now declare loudly…

I AM READY FOR CHANGE!

Soul Searching & Inventory Exercise

Your Strength Is In Your Struggle

Everyone's life is driven by something. Right now, you may be driven by a painful memory, a problem, your past, grief, and other circumstances. Do not allow your past to control your future – journal your thoughts.

What are you currently grateful for in your life (every day can bring about something new to be grateful for)?

_____

_____

_____

_____

_____

_____

What makes you happy?

_____

_____

_____

_____

_____

_____

What is something that you want to achieve in your lifetime?

_____

_____

_____

_____

_____

Write your obituary – What do you want to be remembered for?

_____

_____

_____

_____

_____

What is holding you back in life? And how can you move past these things?

_____

_____

_____

_____

_____

YOUR STRENGTH IS IN YOUR STRUGGLE

Write about what you can do to start taking action towards living a purpose-driven life?

_____

_____

_____

_____

_____

Dear God,

I come to you, in the name of Jesus, thanking you for loving me the way you do. My destiny is in you.

Give me the strength when I am weak. There are times I feel rejected, alone, and in turmoil. Grant me the courage, and the serenity, to accept the things I cannot change.

Courage to change the things I can. And wisdom to know the difference. Fill me Oh Lord, with your light and love. Help me to not lose faith in you.

I know there are times when my faith waivers. There are times when I feel helpless, hopeless, and defenseless.

I need you to rescue me out of my distress. Today, I release my life into your hands as you propel me into my destiny in the name of Jesus – Amen

Chapter 8

Daily Declarations!

My prayer, and desire, for you is that you aspire to greatness without blame, shame, or question. You can do it! You may have doubted yourself, regretted your choices, and ignored your progress. Don't beat up on yourself for your mistakes. The series of hurts you experienced were not designed to destroy you. They are blessings in disguise. Be devoted today to acknowledge that it's time to pack your bags and move on. You are no longer bitter, you are better!

It is said that it takes twenty-one days to break an old habit, or to start a new one. I challenge you to make a commitment to offer yourself the love and acceptance you need to move yourself beyond your past and the failures that have held you back. Be devoted to honor yourself for all the lessons you have learned along the way. Remember to celebrate even the smallest wins, and forgive yourself for the offenses you have committed against yourself. Forgive all those who abused you. Seriously, take a deep breath and LET IT GO! Don't forget to ask the Holy Spirit to lead you on the path that is beneficial for you. Keep pressing forward, trusting God, and believing that all things are possible.

I have included a list of declarations that you can use during your twenty-one days of metamorphosis. As you speak out these declarations, do so prayerfully and with confidence. Ask the Holy Spirit to help you as you exercise your faith. As you read through the declarations, don't merely read them, speak them with faith, and your authority in God will cause your life to be transformed.

DAILY DECLARATIONS

- I decree and declare that my day will be greeted with favor, and that I will be victorious in Jesus Name. I decree that my days, months, and years will be filled with God's glory.

- I decree and declare that I am anointed and appointed for this season, that God will give me strength for every battle, wisdom for every decision, and the peace that passes all understanding.

- I decree and declare supernatural breakthroughs over my life. That God will make me the head and not the tail, above and not beneath, and that I will soar on wings like eagles.

- I decree and I declare that I will walk in prophetic fulfilment, and that I will have what it takes to fulfil my God given calling and assignment.

- I decree and I declare that I choose to move from believing to expecting. I will reach for better than where I am presently. I will pursue my dreams, and goals, in my quest to become a better me.

- I decree and I declare that I will remain focused. That I will pursue a closer relationship with God and walk in total obedience to His Word, constantly looking for ways to improve my life.

- I decree and I declare, starting from today, that I will take the limits off my life, and I will commit to walk in a season of blessings, favor, and prosperity.

- I decree and declare that I will experience God's goodness, and faithfulness, over my life. I will become everything God created me to be.

- I decree and declare that this is my season to soar. God is about to release upon me a supernatural anointing to accomplish my dreams.

- I decree and declare that my life will reflect excellence and integrity. God's favor will overflow my life in abundance.

- I decree and declare that God will open supernatural doors that will usher me into a new season of blessings and growth.

- I decree and declare that the blessings of the Lord will make rich and add no sorrow to my life.

- I decree and declare that no weapon formed against me shall ever prosper because the Lord is on my side.

- I decree and declare that I am blessed in my going out and my coming in. Goodness and mercy will always follow me.

- I decree and declare that my mind is filled with good thoughts. No obstacles can destroy me because my mind is focused on victory.

- I decree and declare breakthroughs are coming into my life. I will rise above every difficulty, because God has given me the power to succeed over my enemies.

- I decree and declare transformation in my mind, body, soul, and spirit.

- I decree and declare that my season of frustration is over

- I decree and declare that I have the DNA of a winner.

- I decree and declare that I am a victor and never a victim.

THIS IS MY DECLARATION

SIGNED:_____ **DATED:**_____

ABOUT THE AUTHOR

"YOU HAVE WHAT IT TAKES TO BE A WINNER NEVER LET GO OF YOUR DREAMS"

A respected leader; equipped with powerful communication and life development skills, Sonia Whitlock has created tremendous impact for more than twenty-five years. She brings hope, healing, and deliverance to thousands of people. A graduate of the Washington International University, and the Caribbean Nazarene College, she obtained multiple degrees in Psychology/Counselling & Theology, Sociology, and Business Administration.

Sonia is a pastor, motivational speaker, life coach, counsellor, author, and recording artist. She has also founded Kaylah's Kids Academy Early Childhood Care, where she mentors children. Whitlock has been an inspirational role model for adolescent girls and women; equipping, motivating, empowering, and inspiring these individuals to reach their maximum potential. Her greatest passion is to see women recognize the power they hold in their mind, body, soul, and spirit – thus enabling them to make informed choices.

Reverend Whitlock has focused her recent efforts in birthing, establishing, and building a state-of-the-art church and youth transformation centre which God has called her to lead, called "Sanctuary of Praise," as she spreads the good news of Jesus Christ to the people of Trinidad, Tobago, and around the world.

She is the proud mother of Keyler and Keylon, and the grandmother of Kaylah, Kylee, and Kes-Ariya. She loves and adores her darling husband Keymer: "The best gift that God can give any woman is the gift of a loving family," she expressed.

Acknowledgement

There are so many people who invested in the development of this project who must be and should be acknowledged. Without them, I would not have been able to meet the stringent demands of my life and still provide the quality writing that was essential to touch the lives of my readers.

I give praise and thanks to Almighty God for giving me the wisdom and the creativity to write this project. For His blessings that makes rich and adds no sorrow to my life. Thank you Lord for loving me the way you do!

My sincere gratitude to my husband Keymer, who supported me during this project. Your enthusiasm, encouragement, wisdom and for believing in me. Your love always brings the highest truth along with it, as we see God in each other.

Keyler and Keylon, I couldn't have children any more wonderful than both of you. Thank you for taking care of me. You always know exactly what I need, exactly when I need it. I am so grateful to have you in my life.

Kaylah, Kylee and Kes-Ariya – You mean the world to me.

To my parents Wilton and Roselyn Nancis, for the love and spiritual upbringing you instilled in me, thus enabling me to become a God-fearing woman of excellence and integrity. I am forever grateful.

To my brother and sisters: Jenny, Linda, Sharon, Wilton (Jnr.) and Marva for your encouragement and your belief in me.

To Dara Publishing LLC, whose genuine love, support and guidance never ceases to amaze me.

ACKNOWLEDGEMENT

Petrina Balfour Sealy, my best friend and spiritual sister – I am certain that God personally sent you to me. Thank you for your diligence and commitment to our friendship and ministry.

My Gratitude to Josanne Rojas and to all my mentors and individuals whose lives I was able to touch. Thank you for believing in my message.

To those who stood in opposition and adversity throughout my journey – thank you. You have enabled me to discover how great God is and who I am in Him. You positioned me!

www.ingramcontent.com/pod-product-compliance
Lightning Source LLC
LaVergne TN
LVHW051250080426
835513LV00016B/1842